LIBRARY
UNIVERSITY LU
1020 S. HAR
EAST LANSING, MI 48823

W9-CGK-782

Be an Angel

Heavenly Hints for Angelic Acts from Your Guardian Spirits

Text by
Dana Reynolds

Illustrations by
Karen Blessen

Simon & Schuster
New York London Toronto Sydney Tokyo Singapore

This book is dedicated to the potential angel in each of us.

SIMON & SCHUSTER

Rockefeller Center
1230 Avenue of the Americas
New York, New York 10020

Copyright © 1994 by Dana Reynolds and Karen Blessen

All rights reserved including the right of reproduction
in whole or in part in any form.

SIMON & SCHUSTER and colophon are registered trademarks
of Simon & Schuster Inc.

DESIGNED BY BARBARA M. MARKS

Manufactured in the United States of America

10 9 8 7 6 5 4 3 2 1

Library of Congress Cataloging-in-Publication Data is available.

ISBN: 0-671- 89694-6

ACKNOWLEDGMENTS

Collectively, we would like to thank Patricia Leasure, our editor, for her expertise and loving care throughout this project. Thank you also Linda Cunningham, Meaghan Dowling, Eve Metz, and Barbara Marks. Special thanks to Dean Williamson, our agent, and Jan Miller of Dupree/Miller and Associates for your professional guidance and assurance. And thanks to Brooke Davis for your support.

—DANA REYNOLDS AND KAREN BLESSEN

The process of writing this book was blessed throughout by angels seen and unseen. Thank you to the following "earth" angels in my life: Nadine Palau, the women of Serenity House, Dana Anderson, Nancy Byers, Bette Epstein, Cynthia Mills, Barbara Nichols, and Susan Stahl. Each of you hold a special place in my heart. Deep gratitude to: Mother, Stacey, Sandy, Chris, and Irene. Your energies are in these pages. Special thanks to Amy, Brad, and Jason; you bring light to my life. And to Don, for your love, for believing in the journey, and for giving me my wings.

—DANA REYNOLDS

I began work on the angel illustrations in Texas, and finished them in my childhood bedroom in Nebraska—home with my parents while my dad battled cancer. The worlds of the sublime and life's struggles inevitably spilled together. Thank you, Mom and Dad, for your love, encouragement, and guidance in my life. Special thanks to: Rey, Betsy, Debby, Les and Janelle, Shelley, Sharon, Jody, Lorraine, Vicki Morgan, Susan Puckett, Bob Shema, and William Snyder. You are my voices of confidence. I love you all! Finally, thank you, Kelly, for our life together.

—KAREN BLESSEN

CONTENTS

I. THE ANGELS OF
OUR NATURAL WORLD

II. THE ANGELS OF
OUR DAY

III. **THE ANGELS OF THE PEOPLE IN OUR LIVES**

IV. **THE ANGELS OF SPECIAL NEEDS AND OCCASIONS**

FOREWORD

*A*ngels are receiving a great deal of attention these days. In fact, we seem to be experiencing an angel renaissance. This book was inspired by the angels and written with their careful guidance. It is a compendium of twentieth-century angel mythology created to awaken our contemporary mortal world to the messengers of God who surround us every day. Each angel suggests ways we might make a positive difference in someone's life.

*I*n these pages are the archetypal angels who will accompany us into the next millennium. Strength and gentleness combine to create supernatural beings of courage and compassion. Our higher good is their universal and divine purpose.

*H*owever, their presence raises a question: Why do unspeakable acts of violence and abuse happen when we are surrounded by beings capable of divine intervention and protection? Perhaps in order to receive answers to these questions and the unending guidance available to us from the angelic realm, we must first tune in to their frequency. This means creating time in our busy lives to be still, to go within, to pray and meditate. The angels are imploring us to protect and savor the beauty around us, and to use all of our senses, talents, and creativity as we move through each day. The virtues of patience, understanding, and loving-kindness combined with the actions of awareness, outreach, and responsibility, create a climate for positive change in our lives.

*W*e must also remember a simple truth. The angels are messengers from God. They carry out their missions by following instructions from the divine. We mortals are not privy to all the secrets of heaven. There are now, as there have always been, great mysteries as to why things happen as they do. This is where individual faith and trust in a higher power sustains and nurtures the soul.

*I*t is interesting to imagine new dominions of angels being established to assist our birth into the next century. Could it be possible that we are being called to become a band of earth angels to work alongside our heavenly friends? If so, we are being presented an opportunity to grow in love and grace. This opening in time, if we choose to explore it, could truly be a gift from the angels.

INTRODUCTION

*L*ong ago, in the heavens, angels were given specific missions for the betterment of humankind and the world we mortals live in. They were chosen for their work according to their individual characteristics and unique talents. These glistening supernatural beings listened carefully to the voice that gave them their assignments. Each angel was adorned with garments to signify the work which had been assigned. Their ordination was followed by a heavenly celebration and a prayerful descent to earth by moonlight.

*G*ently they moved into the world with special graces and an eagerness to impart beauty, love, and kindness. As the angels' sensitivity to the needs of the world developed and they responded with benevolence and caring, they earned their wings, a sign that their work was blessed.

Angels are present in today's world also. This book is a guide to knowing the angels. It reveals to you the many angels who surround you every day. You will learn their names, their characteristics, and their missions. Perhaps you will recognize an angel you have encountered in nature, on the street, while traveling, or in your home.

You will also discover within these pages ways you can be an angel and spread heavenly joy wherever you go. Turn the page to become acquainted with the angels who brighten the world. Look around you for your opportunity to be an angel!

Around our pillows golden ladders rise,

And up and down the skies,

With winged sandals shod,

The angels come and go, the Messengers of God!

—RICHARD HENRY STODDARD

THE ANGELS OF OUR NATURAL WORLD

THE GUARDIANS OF THE NATURAL WORLD ARE
CONSTANTLY MOVING ABOUT OUR PLANET.
EACH ONE IS DIVINELY GUIDED AND DESIGNED
TO FULFILL A SPECIAL MISSION.
THESE ARE THE ANGELS WHO CARE FOR
MOTHER EARTH AND HER ANIMAL KINGDOM.

WINSUM
THE ANGEL OF NATURE

RUMPEL
THE ANGEL OF PETS

BLOOM
THE ANGEL OF THE GARDEN

ETERNAL
THE ANGEL OF THE OCEANS

WINSUM

THE ANGEL OF NATURE

Winsum is Mother Nature's helper. He travels with her through the changing seasons. His wings are shaped like the butterfly's and his voice is gentle, like the lark's. All the colors of the rainbow create his aura.

In spring he guides the birds to safe nesting places and scatters flower seeds wherever he travels. He carries the scent of honeysuckle through open windows and assists the newborn animals into the world.

Summer finds Winsum tying tassels on the corn in the garden and whispering plans for sand castles to children on the beach. In the evenings he lights the fireflies and inspires human imaginations with his cloud designs as they move across the moon.

The autumn is a busy time for Winsum. He awakens Jack Frost and shakes the acorns from the trees for squirrels to carry to their pantries. He reminds the leaves it's time to change colors and he shows the animals where to snuggle in for the cold months ahead.

In the winter Winsum shows the birds and beasts where to find food. He helps design the snowflakes and sends the smell of pine and cedar up chimneys from burning logs.

Winsum, the angel of nature, is nurturer and guardian to all creatures and growing things, the angel made of rainbow light.

BE AN ANGEL OF NATURE

WINSUM'S NAME IS
DERIVED FROM HIS
TWO FAVORITE
SEASONS, WINTER
AND SUMMER.

"COME FORTH INTO
THE LIGHT OF
THINGS, LET
NATURE BE YOUR
TEACHER."
—WILLIAM
WORDSWORTH

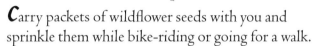

*C*arry packets of wildflower seeds with you and sprinkle them while bike-riding or going for a walk.

*H*ang birdhouses and put out nesting materials in the spring.

*R*ead about The Nature Conservancy.

*S*pread birdseed in the winter or hang feeders near your windows. Remember fresh water for your feathered friends.

BE AN ANGEL OF NATURE

*T*ie bundles of twigs and kindling you find while walking on an autumn afternoon and leave them on the doorstep of a friend's house.

*L*ate at night, take the hand of someone you love, someone who may be feeling blue, go outdoors, and look up at the constellations.

*F*ill tiny baskets with seasonal gatherings from nature as potpourri for angel gifts throughout the year.

"IN ALL THINGS OF NATURE THERE IS SOMETHING OF THE MARVELOUS."
—ARISTOTLE

CONTEMPLATE THE MIRACLES OF NATURE: THE RAINBOW, THE SNOWFLAKE, THE SUNRISE.

BE AN ANGEL OF NATURE

*W*hile walking through the forest, along the beach, or in your neighborhood, pick up litter and dispose of it or recycle it appropriately.

WINSUM LOVES DANCING WITH FALLING SNOWFLAKES!

*T*each a child how to build sand castles on a summer afternoon.

*T*read lightly when walking through the forest. Every inch around, above, and below you is someone's home.

CELEBRATE THE CHANGING SEASONS.

*A*s evening approaches, invite an elderly friend to join you to watch the glorious sunset on the horizon.

UMPEL

THE
ANGEL
OF
PETS

Rumpel, in his patterned coat of spots and stripes, is the guardian and guide for our animal companions. He speaks many animal languages. This angel converses with the cat as she preens herself in the morning sun on the front porch, and the goldfish as he makes endless circles in his large glass bowl. He comforts the molting parakeet and gently whispers reassurances to the dog as she delivers her first litter of pups.

Rumpel protects our four-legged friends as they cross the streets, and he helps them make their way home when they have wandered too far. The angel of pets also watches over displaced animals, the runts, the

unwanted ones, the castaways.
He visits the shelters and
consoles the patient
creatures waiting for homes.

Rumpel is friend to all pets: the box turtle, the snake,
the field mouse, the hamster. These animals also
recognize Rumpel's presence. He moves through the
world guarding, guiding, and counseling our
companions from the animal kingdom.

BE AN ANGEL TO PETS

APPRECIATE
THE WONDER OF ALL
GOD'S CREATURES.

*B*e playful. Throw the ball, toss the catnip, fling the Frisbee.

*C*hange the fish's water. Wash the puppy's blanket. Clean out the cat's litter box. Change the paper in the parrot's cage. Keep your pet's special space neat and tidy.

*R*emember to give your pet fresh food and water each day. It sounds like a simple request, but in our busy world it's easy to forget our animal friends.

*V*olunteer at your local S.P.C.A.

BE AN ANGEL TO PETS

*M*ake sure your pet is protected if she's outside at night. Dress her with a reflector collar to warn oncoming cars.

*L*ook after the lost dog or cat. Check for identification, run an ad in the Found section of your local paper. Do what you can to help the helpless animal.

*O*ffer to look after a traveling friend's pet. Give the animal tender, loving care and reassure him that his master will return soon.

TAKE A PHOTO OF YOUR PET, FRAME IT, AND INCLUDE IT IN YOUR FAMILY GALLERY.

ST. FRANCIS OF ASSISI IS THE PATRON SAINT OF ANIMALS.

BE AN ANGEL TO PETS

HAVE A BIRTHDAY PARTY FOR YOUR DOG! SEND INVITATIONS TO YOUR DOG'S FRIENDS. CREATE A FESTIVE CAKE FROM PET FOOD, ICE IT WITH SOFTENED CREAM CHEESE PROVIDE PARTY HATS FOR PICTURE TAKING.

*V*isit your local shelter and adopt a pet. Look for that wagging tail, those whiskers, the soulful eyes that say to you: "Take me home. I'll be your faithful companion."

*G*ive your dog or kitty a massage. It has been observed that gentle stroking of a pet, while thinking quieting thoughts has a calming effect on overly active animals.

*M*ost of all, love your pet. In return you'll get wet kisses, a welcoming pounce when you come home, and a faithful companion from the miraculous animal kingdom.

BLOOM

THE ANGEL OF THE GARDEN

A garment of rose petals and a garland of ivy: garden stuff creates Bloom's vestments. Bloom is the angel of the garden, guardian of the flora and the fauna.

The garden angel directs the honeybees to the juiciest flowers. She guides the ivy up the stone wall and she makes a wish as she blows the dandelion that has turned to seed.

Bloom is an excellent teacher. She instructs mother birds on how to build their first nests, and consoles them when all too soon their young spread their wings and fly away.

The busy angel Bloom respectfully asks the garden snail to dine elsewhere and she's always available to help a budding flower unfold. The rabbits lead Bloom on a merry chase, and the butterflies appreciate her help as they emerge from their cocoons.

In the evenings Bloom says vespers with the praying mantis and later plays tag with the fireflies. Her fingernails are dirty and her thumbs are green. She is a hardworking spirit.

If you discover webworms some sunny Saturday morning, just call on Bloom. You'll know she's about when you see the dandelions blow.

BE AN ANGEL IN THE GARDEN

SUPPORT YOUR
COMMUNITY PARK
OR BOTANICAL
GARDEN WITH YOUR
TIME, MONEY, OR
BOTH.

*U*se organic insect repellents and fertilizers. Stock your garden with praying mantis. They are beautiful to observe and are natural exterminators for unwanted pests.

*P*lant zinnias, sunflowers, marigolds, morning glories to support the butterflies and honeybees. Include fennel and dill to attract black swallowtail butterflies.

*J*oin a gardening organization. Learn about your local ecology.

CREATE A ROCK
GARDEN WITHIN A
FLOWER BED. USE IT
AS A QUIET PLACE
FOR MEDITATION.

BE AN ANGEL IN THE GARDEN

*S*hare a start of a particularly beautiful antique rosebush with your neighbor. Blanket your neighborhood with its beauty and color.

*G*enerously give your surplus tomatoes, cucumbers, herbs, and daisies to a local food pantry.

*C*reate a place for sitting with others to enjoy the beauty and solace of a garden. Tall chilled glasses of lemonade with flower-filled ice cubes complete the moment.

*S*tart a group to plant wildflowers in your neighborhood.

TEND, NURTURE, AND APPRECIATE WHAT YOU'VE PLANTED. TAKE THE TIME TO REALLY LOOK AT A BLOSSOM, OR A BEE, OR A HUMMINGBIRD.

BE AN ANGEL IN THE GARDEN

*H*ang wind chimes to make music for your garden's creatures.

*B*uild a big, glorious compost bin and watch as your grass clippings and fall leaves metamorphose into a rich, lush, natural fertilizer.

OUTSIDE THE OPEN
WINDOW
THE MORNING AIR
IS ALL AWASH WITH
ANGELS.
—RICHARD PURDY
WILBUR

*P*lant wisely, giving thought to what grows best where you live.

ETERNAL

THE

ANGEL

OF

THE OCEANS

Wings strong and feathered like the gull's carry Eternal over the vastness of the earth's oceans. She is iridescent, sparkling, like the sunfish, and swift as the sandpiper.

Eternal flies above the seas, guardian of Mother Nature's ocean life. She warns the birds of oncoming storms, and she rescues playful sea lion pups caught in a kelp bed.

She reminds the giant turtles when it's time to make their pilgrimage up the beach to bury their eggs. The sea angel can be found diving deep into the oceans to untangle the octopus, and corral the seahorses.

Eternal grieves at the sight of oil slicks and floating refuse. She warns the creatures to stay away and churns the water to restore its clarity.

Our angel of the oceans dances on the surf, and waves to her companion Sister Moon, the keeper of the tides. Eternal sings with the dolphin and the whale and sprinkles shells and other sea gifts along the sand for a beachcomber's bounty.

The next time you are walking along the seashore and you hear the sound of gull wings, yet no birds are in sight, it may be the ocean angel, Eternal, making her rounds. You will recognize her as the sparkle on the incoming tide.

BE AN ANGEL TO THE OCEANS

*B*e respectful of the sea's delicate ecology. Observe rather than interact with tide pools and sea creatures.

*W*hen picnicking on the beach, clean up all litter and extinguish beach fires with sand.

*W*hen boating, keep all trash on board to dispose of later. Sea life is threatened by our litter.

*W*hen gathering shells, be selective, not greedy.

*R*ead about organizations such as Save The Whales and Greenpeace. Become educated about ways you can become involved in protecting our oceans.

"SEAS ROLL TO WAFT ME, SUNS TO LIGHT ME RISE; MY FOOTSTOOL EARTH, MY CANOPY THE SKIES."
—ALEXANDER POPE

GO MOONBATHING UNDER SISTER MOON ON A SUMMER NIGHT. OBSERVE HER SILVER LIGHT AS IT RIPPLES ON THE WAVES.

BE AN ANGEL TO THE OCEANS

*C*onserve electricity. Power plants create acid rain, which in turn pollutes the oceans.

*F*or those who live inland, know that insecticides, herbicides, and fertilizers eventually find their way to the ocean. Remember that everything upstream ends up downstream.

*M*editate while sitting on the beach. Listen for angel songs in the crashing surf. If you are landlocked, meditate while listening to a tape of ocean sounds.

*G*ather a sand-castle kit. Include a spray bottle, small shovel, bucket, spoon, gelatin molds, miniature flags, and toy soldiers.

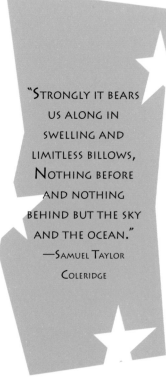

"STRONGLY IT BEARS US ALONG IN SWELLING AND LIMITLESS BILLOWS, NOTHING BEFORE AND NOTHING BEHIND BUT THE SKY AND THE OCEAN."
—SAMUEL TAYLOR COLERIDGE

II
THE ANGELS OF OUR DAY

ANGELS CONSTANTLY SURROUND US.
WELCOME OUR BLESSED COMPANIONS, WHO
SUPPORT AND GUIDE US AS WE GO ABOUT
OUR DAILY LIVES. BECOME ACQUAINTED WITH
THE ANGELS OF OUR DAY.

*A*BIDE
THE ANGEL OF THE HOME

*W*ISDOM
THE ANGEL OF THE SCHOOL

*C*ARRY
THE ANGEL OF THE FREEWAYS

*H*ARMONY
THE ANGEL OF THE WORKPLACE

BIDE

Abide, the resident angel, is the spirit who keeps the home fires burning and welcomes you in from the storm. His robe is made from a patchwork quilt and he wears lamb's-wool slippers on his feet. The glow from his halo provides a night light for midnight raids on the refrigerator.

A gentle tap on the head from a falling tennis racket is a signal from Abide that it's time to clean the hall closet. This is a fastidious angel, and helping us to be organized is part of his job description.

Abide creates welcoming energy in a variety of living spaces. Apartments, condos, houses, and mobile homes provide the backgrounds for his duties to be carried out.

After you have spent a long, hard day in the busy world, the angel of the house sends the message, "It's time to go home." He encourages you to heave a deep sigh as your key unlocks the door and you take off your shoes. This angel welcomes the weary and signals approaching sleep by inviting a long yawn.

Abide is an expert guardian and comforter. He reminds you to lock the doors before going to bed, and he whispers to you to pull the covers tight during a thunderstorm, while he chases away nightmares.

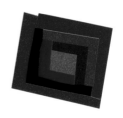

In the morning Abide makes sure the alarm clock signals a new day, and he directs the aroma of brewing coffee all through the house. You'll know Abide the next time you are about to leave your home and an inner voice says, "You'd better close the upstairs window—it may rain today." Abide, creator of comfort and guardian of the house.

BE AN ANGEL IN YOUR HOME

*P*ut loving, caring energy into your home. Oil the squeaky door, paint the scuffed hallway, clean out the garage.

*C*reate a meditation space for yourself in the corner of your bedroom or living room. Fill this space with a comfy chair or pillows, candles, your favorite books, music, fresh flowers. Let your home be a haven in your busy life.

*I*f you live in an apartment, be respectful of your neighbors. Close doors quietly and keep noise to a minimum.

MILLIONS OF SPIRITUAL CREATURES WALK THE EARTH UNSEEN, BOTH WHEN WE WAKE, AND WHEN WE SLEEP.
—JOHN MILTON

BE AN ANGEL IN YOUR HOME

*R*ecycle newspapers, glass, and aluminum. You can help the planet by beginning at home.

*P*ass along furnishings and appliances you no longer need or use to make someone else's life more comfortable.

*B*e a good neighbor. To help an elderly or ill neighbor, place their newspaper near their front door. Save them unnecessary steps.

*F*ill your home with music. Allow music to enhance the desired mood. Everything from peaceful (Debussy) to festive (folk tunes).

ABIDE'S DEFINITION OF HOME: A WELCOMING ENVIRONMENT CREATED WITH LOVE. THE PLACE YOU LONG TO BE AT THE END OF THE DAY.

BE AN ANGEL IN YOUR HOME

Create a comfortable place where you and a friend can have tea, cookies, and a golden conversation.

SIGHTS THAT BRING A SMILE TO ABIDE'S FACE:
—CHILDREN TUCKED SNUG IN THEIR BEDS AFTER A GOODNIGHT KISS.
—THE FAMILY SHARING A SIMPLE MEAL AT THE KITCHEN TABLE.
—A HOUSEHOLD CUDDLED SNUG AND WARM AROUND THE FIRE.

A FAVORITE RECIPE FROM ABIDE'S KITCHEN: ANGEL CLOUD PARFAIT

IN A LARGE BOWL COMBINE 1-INCH SQUARES OF ANGEL FOOD CAKE, WHIPPED CREAM FLAVORED WITH A TINY DROP OR TWO OF PEPPERMINT EXTRACT, AND CHOCOLATE CHIPS. FILL TALL, FANCY PARFAIT GLASSES WITH THIS MIXTURE. DRIZZLE THE TOP WITH CHOCOLATE SYRUP AND ADD A DOLLOP OF WHIPPED CREAM. SERVE ON A DESSERT PLATE COVERED WITH A PAPER DOILY THAT HAS BEEN SPRINKLED WITH TINY SILVER STARS.

ISDOM

THE
ANGEL
OF
THE SCHOOL

Wisdom's wings are fashioned like the owl's. He is an educated angel and he is never without his book of knowledge. He uses it for reference only, because Wisdom is a scholar and a sage.

Wisdom is found in school and university libraries guiding students to helpful resources. He calms the jittery nerves of test takers by boosting their confidence with a whispered answer to the first question.

The angel of the school is also a friend and supporter of the teachers. His mission is to be an intermediary between the educators and the students. Wisdom is there to celebrate the great "aha" when a pupil's mind is brightened by the light of understanding.

This scholarly angel can calculate numbers in a millisecond, spell words in every spoken language, and recall dates from history since time began. He works long hours into the night supporting the college freshman challenged by her first semester. He is just as comfortable reciting Shakespeare with the postgraduate as he is repeating the ABC's with the kindergartner.

Wisdom is found wherever mortals search for higher learning. The angel of the school provides inspiration to the seeker, the human on a quest for understanding and enlightenment. Wisdom understands that there are many ways of assimilating information. Sometimes knowledge is gained through experience. Wisdom is often found in the school of hard knocks. He finds this his most challenging work. This particular way of learning is experienced on our city streets, in our workplaces, and often within our own homes. Wisdom is especially supportive of the students of the school of hard knocks, for he knows that the lessons learned here are life lessons.

You know Wisdom is nearby if you suddenly develop a new interest or discover a hidden talent. This is the angel who believes you're never too old to learn.

BE AN ANGEL TO SCHOOLS

EXPAND YOUR
MIND BY LEARNING
SOMETHING NEW.
EXPAND SOMEONE
ELSE'S MIND BY
SHARING YOUR
KNOWLEDGE.

LISTEN TO THE
ELDERLY. THEY ARE
TEACHERS WITH A
LIFETIME OF
EXPERIENCE.

*B*e open to life as a school where you continue to learn. Every experience offers an opportunity for self-expansion.

*C*reate an atmosphere of playful learning in your home. Honor a child's creativity by displaying her artwork in a hallway gallery.

*V*olunteer for the P.T.A. Be an involved parent in all aspects of your child's education.

*L*earn something new! Attend a reading of Russian poetry or an art history lecture.

BE AN ANGEL TO SCHOOLS

Start a study group or a book club. Select a topic or book and gather a group of friends together at your home, library, or coffeehouse and discuss each individual's perspective on the material.

Volunteer at a local home for the elderly. Read, teach a craft, or hold a sing-along. Remember, you're never to old to learn.

Make a gift of a special magazine, a book of poetry or a classic novel. Provide intellectual stimulation.

Create a family bulletin board as a place to share poetry, interesting articles, or something new you learned today.

"PREJUDICES, IT IS WELL KNOWN, ARE MOST DIFFICULT TO ERADICATE FROM THE HEART WHOSE SOIL HAS NEVER BEEN LOOSENED OR FERTILIZED BY EDUCATION; THEY GROW THERE, FIRM AS WEEDS AMONG STONES."
—CHARLOTTE BRONTË

BE AN ANGEL TO SCHOOLS

BEGIN A VOCABULARY JOURNAL. WHILE READING, JOT DOWN WORDS YOU'RE UNFAMILIAR WITH. LATER REFER TO THE DICTIONARY FOR THE DEFINITION AND RECORD IT IN YOUR JOURNAL.

*E*ncourage a child's curiosity. Talk about what makes the sky blue and what makes the grass grow.

*F*oster an attitude of acceptance and interest in other cultures and belief systems.

*B*ooks are just one way of learning. Ask someone to teach you a craft, a language, a cooking method. Take a class, join a club, rent a teaching video. There are countless ways to learn.

*T*each the young people in your life through shared experiences. Plant seeds together, build together, paint and draw together. Nurture young, creative minds.

CARRY

Carry is dressed for duty. She wears an aluminum helmet, her gown is covered with reflectors, and her sunglasses are wraparounds. The light from her halo goes from bright to dim. Her wings are compact and scratch resistant, and she totes a spare tire on her back.

This angel with nerves of steel is able to weave in and out among the cars, trucks, motorcycles, and vans that endlessly move along our highways. She escorts the traffic-reporting helicopters and from her bird's-eye view watches for potential accidents and gridlocks.

Carry is the angel who calms the nervous motorist stuck on the interstate, late for his meeting. She knows this is a potential mishap-producing situation.

In the middle of the night the angel of the road is found riding alongside the sleepy truck driver. She creates the aroma of a cheeseburger and coffee in his cab, and puts a gurgle in his belly. Soon he pulls over to the nearest truck stop for a rest.

Mothers and children are especially dear to Carry. She reminds moms to buckle up their young passengers and also themselves. Often when the mother has had a hard day, Carry sings a lullaby to a fussy baby in the backseat. Soon the little guy is fast asleep, allowing mother to concentrate on getting them home safely in the evening traffic.

If you should find yourself with a flat tire on the interstate, say a little prayer to Carry, and be assured that help is on the way. It just might come in the form of an angel.

BE AN ANGEL ON THE FREEWAYS

The next time you pull up to the tollbooth, tell the attendent you wish to pay for the person behind you too. What a nice surprise for a stranger on her way home.

Play quiet, soothing music while driving when your nerves are jittery. You become a safer driver when you relax.

Use stoplights as an opportunity to take a few deep breaths and count your blessings. Seeing red lights as a chance to focus on something positive can brighten your journey.

LISTEN TO BOOKS ON TAPE WHILE DRIVING. LEARN WHILE YOU DRIVE.

"EASE ON DOWN EASE ON DOWN THE ROAD."
—FROM THE BROADWAY MUSICAL "THE WIZ"

BE AN **A**NGEL ON THE **F**REEWAYS

*I*f you see a motorist in distress, alert the authorities at your first stop.

*K*eep a litter bag inside your car. Litter on the freeways is dangerous and expensive to remove.

*C*arpool when possible. Save gasoline and wear and tear. It's also an opportunity to have stimulating conversations.

*W*hen traveling long distances with pets, exercise them frequently and remember fresh water. Always use a leash when making roadside stops and be sure your pet wears identification.

EVERY CAR NEEDS TO BE PREPARED FOR AN EMERGENCY. CARRY'S EMERGENCY KIT INCLUDES: A STRONG FLASHLIGHT, BATTERIES, FLARES, JUMPER CABLES, A SPARE TIRE, A JACK, A WRENCH, AND A SHOVEL. A FIRST-AID KIT AND ASPIRIN MIGHT ALSO COME IN HANDY.

BE AN ANGEL ON THE FREEWAYS

*T*ake a course in CPR and first aid from the American Red Cross. You could save a life!

*P*ack a "goody" bag for a friend who is going on a journey. Include fruit, cheese and crackers, and chocolate for snacking. Also add a tape of rousing music to keep the weary traveler alert.

*B*e sure that any small child riding in your car is protected by an appropriate car seat.

*V*olunteer to be a designated driver at the next party you attend.

MAKE SURE EVERYONE IS BUCKLED UP BEFORE YOU START YOUR CAR.

JOIN M.A.D.D. (MOTHERS AGAINST DRUNK DRIVING).

ARMONY

The Angel of the Workplace

Harmony is the constantly challenged angel. She is a diplomat, troubleshooter, and mediator extraordinaire! She is dressed for business and her sleeves are rolled up in a professional fashion.

This very busy angel moves throughout the workplace, quieting discords by whispering tactful phrases into the ears of employees. She attends presentations and meetings and inspires self-assured, quick responses to daring questions. She acts as a muse for creative thinking when deadlines are at hand.

Harmony is also comfortable making on-the-spot repairs when the copy machine jams or the water cooler leaks. She finds missing pens, reports, and resources and delivers them to the one in need.

The office is not the only place where Harmony is found. Construction sites, operating rooms, restaurants—all are homes to the angel of the workplace. Wherever folks are on the job, she is there. She rescues the workman's lunch box as it teeters on scaffolding. It's Harmony who ensures the surgical nurse is alert and quick-thinking. And of course she's the one who keeps the kitchen calm during the evening dinner rush at the local diner.

This is the angel who gives a boost to the weary, by inspiring a co-worker to pay a compliment or write a note of appreciation. Harmony keeps the coffee hot and tempers cool. She is found working late at night alongside those doing overtime. This is the angel whose name is her goal. Harmony in the workplace.

BE AN ANGEL IN THE WORKPLACE

"WORK BANISHES
THOSE THREE
GREAT EVILS,
BOREDOM, VICE,
AND POVERTY."
—VOLTAIRE

HARMONY GLOWS
WITH PRIDE WHEN
SHE HEARS A BOSS
COMPLIMENT A JOB
WELL DONE.

*L*eave an "angel note" on the water cooler or vending machine saying, "Take a deep breath, move peacefully through your day."

*C*arry small wrapped candies in your pocket to give as "angel kisses" to someone who needs a lift.

*O*nce a month, leave copies of an inspirational poem or thought on your co-workers' desks.

*B*ring a cake to celebrate all the "non-birthdays" in your workplace.

BE AN ANGEL IN THE WORKPLACE

*B*undle up any perfume or lotion samples you've received. Wrap the bundle in pretty paper and attach an "angel note" saying, "This is for the first person who finds this, just to brighten your day." Leave the package in the restroom.

*H*elp to put out the fires of gossip where you work by not spreading rumors.

CREATE A "GOOD NEWS" BULLETIN BOARD IN YOUR WORKPLACE. MAKE IT A PLACE TO SHARE THE GOOD NEWS OF THE PEOPLE YOU WORK WITH: PHOTOS OF A NEW BABY, AN ARTICLE ABOUT A SPECIAL HONOR RECEIVED, OR INFORMATION ABOUT AN EXCITING COMING EVENT.

> "WORK IS LOVE MADE VISIBLE. AND IF YOU CANNOT WORK WITH LOVE BUT ONLY WITH DISTASTE, IT IS BETTER THAT YOU SHOULD LEAVE YOUR WORK AND SIT AT THE GATE OF THE TEMPLE AND TAKE ALMS OF THOSE WHO WORK WITH JOY."
> —KAHLIL GIBRAN

III
THE ANGELS OF THE PEOPLE IN OUR LIVES

FROM MORNING TO NIGHT WE INTERACT WITH FAMILY,
FRIENDS, CO-WORKERS, AND OTHERS WHO CROSS OUR PATHS.
ANGELS OFTEN ACT AS ORCHESTRATORS IN THE CREATION
AND DEVELOPMENT OF OUR RELATIONSHIPS WITH ONE ANOTHER.
IN THIS CHAPTER YOU WILL BE INTRODUCED TO:

GRACE
THE ANGEL OF MOTHERS

TENDER
THE ANGEL OF THE BELOVED

WORTHY
THE ANGEL OF FATHERS

FOSTER
THE ANGEL OF THE PASSERSBY

JOY
THE ANGEL OF CHILDREN

PRECIOUS
THE ANGEL OF FRIENDS

GRACE

THE

ANGEL

OF

MOTHERS

Grace speaks with a calm and reassuring voice. Her guidance is something mothers grow to count on. Her wings are small and feminine, yet strong and resilient. She wears her long, copper-colored hair in a single braid, and her aura shines like the sun. Her countenance is reassuring and dependable. Grace is a beacon for mothers everywhere. Her energy is transmitted at the speed of light to the mother in need of guidance and support.

The angel of mothers is a friend and companion. She is present at the first stirrings of motherhood. It is Grace who stays nearby during pregnancy and birth. She keeps the new mother company during weary middle of the night feedings, and shares the joyful moment when baby takes her first steps.

Grace is there on the job to comfort the mother who has a child at day care for the first time. She gives a second wind to the tired mother as she drives away from the office to begin her evening tasks at home. She teaches balance to the working mother to help her juggle the responsibilities of career and family.

Grace, the angel of mothers, is more than a nine-to-five angel. Because, just like the mothers she supports, hers is an around-the-clock job. At night, she prays with the mother waiting for her teenager to return home safely from a party. In the morning she spreads her wings around the mother tending a sick child. When a child has grown up and moved away, it is Grace who offers comfort to the mother with an empty nest.

Grace reminds mom to play and savor the precious time of motherhood. She is a comforter, guide, and helpmate. She blesses mothers with patience, understanding, and Grace.

BE AN ANGEL TO MOTHERS

*O*ffer to relieve a new mother for a couple of hours so she can have an evening out.

*C*all your mother and tell her you love her. Treat her to a movie she's been wanting to see.

MOTHERLY
GRACES IMPARTED
BY GRACE:
—PATIENCE
—UNDERSTANDING
—UNCONDITIONAL
LOVE

*O*n a child's first day of school, take her mother to lunch.

*C*elebrate a friend's pregnancy by giving her a journal to record her thoughts and feelings in during the experience.

BE AN ANGEL TO MOTHERS

*T*ake your mother to one of her favorite places. Tell her it's to celebrate that she's your mom.

*O*ne afternoon while baby-sitting a friend's child, take a few photos. Frame them and surprise your friend.

*P*ut a colorful bag filled with magazines, candy, bath salts, etc., on the front porch for a mom who has cabin fever.

*S*end a letter to your mother-in-law. Tell her you love her too.

A MOTHER'S PRAYER FOR HER TEENAGER: PROTECT AND GUIDE HER DAY AND NIGHT. BLESS HER WITH GOOD JUDGMENT AND A FLEXIBLE MIND. HELP HER TO GROW IN GRACE AND WISDOM. AMEN.

BE AN ANGEL TO MOTHERS

*M*ake your mother a scrapbook of her life, beginning when she was a child up to the present time. Remind her how beautiful she was . . . and still is.

*C*reate a celebration when a friend's child takes that first step, says the first word, or lands a scholarship to college.

*O*n your mom's birthday, plan a luncheon for her with her friends. Surprise her with all the trimmings, flowers, gifts, and plenty of time to make her feel very special.

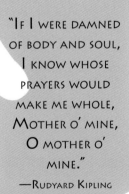

"IF I WERE DAMNED
OF BODY AND SOUL,
I KNOW WHOSE
PRAYERS WOULD
MAKE ME WHOLE,
MOTHER O' MINE,
O MOTHER O'
MINE."
—RUDYARD KIPLING

WORTHY

The Angel of Fathers

Strong shoulders and a compassionate heart are Worthy's trademarks. Strength and tenderness combine to create the angel of fathers. These are the same qualities she strives to deliver to dads the world over. Her wings are large and flexible and she has a warm laugh to match her sense of humor.

Fathers with children of all ages can count on Worthy. She is there to support the dad who must use tough love with an adolescent in crisis. Discipline radiating from compassion and understanding is Worthy's goal.

The new father is encouraged by Worthy to take an active role in the care of his infant. She reassures the nervous dad as he bathes his slippery newborn for the

first time. Soon father and baby are cuddled together, enjoying each other's company.

Worthy can be found in offices and airports all over the world comforting the father who is missing a school program, or his child's first words. She smiles at the joy of seeing a dad share his precious time to mentor his son or play catch with his daughter.

Worthy is an angel in residence for the long haul. She is there to help the dad who coaches the Little League team, and to fortify the father of the bride. Patience and understanding are virtues near and dear to Worthy. The angel of fathers teaches dad to let go, so that he might appreciate the uniqueness of his child.

The angel of fathers is always reassuring, guiding, and supporting, and teaches fathers that they are truly Worthy.

BE AN ANGEL TO FATHERS

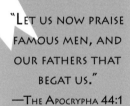

"LET US NOW PRAISE FAMOUS MEN, AND OUR FATHERS THAT BEGAT US."
—THE APOCRYPHA 44:1

There may come a time when you will be called upon to see to your aging father's care. As your childhood memories wash over you, meet this challenge with courage and love. Worthy is asking you to return to your dad the energy and time he once gave to you.

Make a "You're a Father!" bag for a new dad. Fill it with bubble-gum cigars to hand out to friends; a picture frame for baby's first photo; a book of lullabies so he'll be able to soothe the little guy; and a night light for midnight changings.

BE AN ANGEL TO FATHERS

Collect memorabilia from your childhood and put together a memory book for your dad. Let him know how he played an important part in your development.

Dads get taken for granted sometimes. They work hard, saving money for their child's future at a time when the child may not comprehend or appreciate this outpouring of love and energy. It's never too late to say, "Thank you, Dad, for the opportunities you gave me through all your hard work. Now I understand."

IF YOUR FATHER HAS DIED, AND YOU HAVE THINGS YOU'D LIKE TO SAY TO HIM, WRITE HIM A LETTER. LET THE ANGELS DELIVER IT.

BE AN ANGEL TO FATHERS

IF YOUR DAD LIVES FAR AWAY, RECORD A LETTER ON TAPE TO SEND TO HIM. IT WILL MAKE HIM SMILE TO HEAR YOUR VOICE AND HE CAN REPLAY IT ANYTIME HE FEELS LONESOME.

WORTHY'S MISSION FOR DADS IN THE TWENTIETH CENTURY:

WORTHY HAS BEEN SENT TO HELP FATHERS SHARE THEIR FEELINGS WITH THEIR CHILDREN AND TO REMEMBER HOW TO BE PLAYFUL. SHE OFFERS FATHERS THE OPPORTUNITY TO BECOME MENTORS AND GUIDES TO THEIR CHILDREN. THIS IS THE TIME FOR FATHERS TO RETURN TO ACTIVE PARENTING, TO SHARE THE JOYS AND RESPONSIBILITIES BEYOND PROVIDING FOR THE PHYSICAL NEEDS OF THEIR SONS AND DAUGHTERS.

JOY

THE ANGEL OF CHILDREN

Joy is a child in angel form, companion to children, pink energy, and starlight. She appears as a cherub, a plump angel, playful, imaginative, and quick-moving.

Joy is invisible to adult eyes, but children always know when she's near. She is their friend and guardian. At the moment of birth, Joy whispers the secrets of heaven into tiny ears. This little angel is creative as she inspires ways to build a city from cardboard boxes. A linguist, Joy shares with children ways to communicate with the animals. And she is particularly adept at chasing away bad dreams and monsters in closets.

Joy is sometimes a trickster. Parents find this disturbing and often blame the child, when in fact it's the angel exercising her mischievous side. You know this cherub is up to her high jinks when your little one gets the giggles at church or puts a rubber spider in Aunt Lucy's iced tea.

Frolicsome she may be, but don't underestimate Joy's sense of duty. She recognizes when there is trouble nearby. This angel is a companion to the lonely child and protector of the soul for the abused child. In a heartbeat, she can create an imaginary world of incredible beauty, an escape hatch and haven from darkness and fear. A creative future is often born from Joy's protection of a child's psyche and spirit through the imagination.

Joy is made of starlight, eternally young, inventive and high-spirited. She is the guardian cherub, the angel of children. She is joyful.

BE AN ANGEL TO CHILDREN

> "I'VE HEARD THAT LITTLE INFANTS CONVERSE BY SMILES AND SIGNS. WITH THE GUARDIAN BAND OF ANGELS THAT ROUND ABOUT THEM SHINES, UNSEEN BY GROSSER SENSES; BELOVED ONE!"
> —CAROLINE ANNE SOUTHEY

*V*olunteer for the March of Dimes, The Children's Defense Fund, or other organizations benefiting children's welfare.

*F*oster self-confidence in a young person. Create an art gallery in your home for a child's artwork. Frame the art in plastic box frames and arrange them on a kitchen wall or in a hallway. The box frames allows the art to change weekly.

*T*each a craft or skill to a child. Share your talent and be ready to see a smiling face.

BE AN ANGEL TO CHILDREN

★

*V*olunteer at a local hospital to help with the newborns. Some hospitals have programs for volunteers to feed and hold infants in need of extra care.

★

*E*ncourage creativity by having a box of "fun scraps" available for young visitors at your house. Collect scrap fabrics, foils, papers, stickers, etc. Provide paper and glue and watch a masterpiece happen!

★

*P*lay with a child and remember your child within.

★

"CHILDREN HAVE MORE NEED OF MODELS THAN OF CRITICS."
—JOSEPH JOUBERT

JOY SAYS, "ALL THE WONDERS OF HEAVEN ARE IN A BABY'S EYES."

BE AN ANGEL TO CHILDREN

Karl Menninger once said, "What's done to children, they will do to society." Help to break the cycle of violence. If you know a child is being abused or neglected, contact the proper authorities.

All human beings thrive on positive guidance. Honest praise and encouragement create a climate for a child's healthy self-image.

Send an angel note to school with your child. Wish him good luck on his math test and tuck the message into his lunch box or school bag.

> IT IS SAID THAT THE INDENTATION BETWEEN THE NOSE AND UPPER LIP IS THE SPACE WHERE AT THE MOMENT OF BIRTH, A CHILD'S GUARDIAN ANGEL PRESSES HER FINGER, SO THE LITTLE ONE WON'T TELL THE SECRETS OF HEAVEN.

TENDER

THE ANGEL OF THE BELOVED

Sensitivity is Tender's most endearing attribute. She is attuned to the physical, emotional, and spiritual needs of the beloved. Tender is a hovering angel. She is bound to humanity by a desire to ignite, nurture, and heal the romantic heart.

Tender is pure candlelight. She has mighty wings of long white feathers, and her diaphanous garment sparkles as though covered by diamond dust. Her eyes are the color of moonlight on a deep blue sea, and a mane of golden hair frames her delicate face. She is the angel of love. She is the angel of passion. She is the angel of the human heart.

Tender tends the hearts of those in love, and those who

grieve the loss of love. The angel of the beloved connects lovers through dreams and nighttime visions. Chance meetings, coincidental happenings, are Tender's ways of partaking in romantic destiny.

When a romance has ended, the candlelight angel brings comfort to the lonely. She folds her warm, soft wings around the broken heart and applies her celestial balm to wounds from unrequited love. Tender floods the eyes with tears to soothe the pain of the forgotten lover.

Happier moments find the angel of the beloved watching over the bride and groom, and filling the air with the smell of roses on their wedding day. At dusk, she rekindles the fires of passion in a marriage sustained by glowing embers. And when a couple is parted by death, Tender keeps the one on earth company with memories of sun-kissed days and cozy nights with their beloved.

The sound of violins and bells, the aroma of a garden full of flowers, and a feeling of lightness are Tender's trademarks. The next time you sense a fragrance of gardenias and hear the faint tinkling of tiny chimes, observe the candlelight. Know that your beloved is somewhere near, and Tender is the night.

BE AN ANGEL TO YOUR BELOVED

*S*tart a lovers' journal. In a blank book write a message to your significant other. Use the book as a way to communicate feelings that might otherwise be difficult to express face to face. The only rule is that everything must be expressed in a loving way. This can also be a place to keep poems, letters, cards, etc., from beloved to beloved. Keep it wrapped in a beautiful scarf as something sacred, like the relationship you share.

*S*pend a Saturday doing everything your beloved enjoys doing. Relish in the delight of just being together.

*S*urprise your partner with coffee in bed.

> "LOVE, YOU KNOW, SEEKS TO MAKE HAPPY RATHER THAN TO BE HAPPY."
> —RALPH CONNOR

BE AN ANGEL TO YOUR BELOVED

*I*f you have to be away from home for a few days, leave love notes in places where your beloved will be sure to find them: in a coat pocket, on the car visor, and, of course, under the pillow.

*W*rite a love letter today and send it certified mail to your beloved.

*G*ive your beloved a soothing massage with scented oils such as jasmine or sandalwood.

*W*atch a sunset together, holding hands.

CREATE A LOVER'S SHRINE TO HONOR YOUR RELATIONSHIP. DECORATE A SMALL TABLE WITH A SCARF, FLOWERS, AND CANDLES. EACH PERSON ADDS TOKENS TO REPRESENT THEIR LOVE FOR THE OTHER. PHOTOS, JEWELRY, OR TOUCHSTONES MAY BE ADDED PERIODICALLY.

BE AN ANGEL TO YOUR BELOVED

"THE EVENING STAR, LOVE'S HARBINGER."
—JOHN MILTON

Create a love potion out of 1 part cranberry juice; 1 part lime juice; and 2 parts sparkling apple juice. Freeze nasturtium flowers in an ice-cube tray. Mix the above ingredients together and serve over ice in crystal goblets.

"LOVE CONSISTS IN THIS, THAT TWO SOLITUDES PROTECT AND TOUCH AND GREET EACH OTHER."
—RAINER MARIA RILKE

WRITE YOUR OWN VOWS OF LOVE TO ONE ANOTHER.
EACH ANNIVERSARY OR WHENEVER YOUR HEARTS DESIRE, RENEW YOUR VOWS BY WRITING AN UPDATED VERSION AND READ THEM ALOUD TO ONE ANOTHER. SAVE THESE VOWS OF LOVE AND COMMITMENT IN A BOOK AND KEEP THEM BY YOUR BEDSIDE.

FOSTER

THE ANGEL OF THE PASSERSBY

Foster's mission is to prompt serendipitous acts of sharing, generosity, and assistance throughout each day. All angels practice these activities regardless of their heavenly missions. Foster, however, is among us to provide the opportunity to reach out to our fellow mortals through kindness and consideration.

This industrious angel is small and quick-moving. His aura is composed of a rainbow of vibrating colors to complement the ever-changing stream of humanity he interacts with. The angel of the passersby is also known as the angel of smiles. Foster's smile is his most endearing feature. He encourages grinning between mortals while imparting laughter and a sense of humor.

 The smiling angel is found in supermarkets, on city streets, in taxi queues, and elevators. He whispers kindness into the hearts and minds of hustling, bustling men and women.

Foster is present when we allow someone in a hurry to move ahead of us in line. He helps us have the eyes to notice an elderly woman who needs a smiling soul to help her open a heavy door.

The angel of the passersby reminds us that we are on a collective journey through space and time. He is present to show us that the healing of the planet can begin with a kind word and an outstretched hand. The angel of smiles has come to Foster open eyes and caring hearts.

BE AN ANGEL TO PASSERSBY

> "LET BROTHERLY
> LOVE CONTINUE.
> BE NOT FORGETFUL
> TO ENTERTAIN
> STRANGERS:
> FOR THEREBY SOME
> HAVE ENTERTAINED
> ANGELS UNAWARES."
> —HEBREWS 13:1-2

*W*hen shopping at the supermarket, leave coupons you can't use on the appropriate shelf. Let another shopper benefit from your anonymous act of kindness.

*A*s you move throughout your day, open your eyes to those around you. Notice the left-behind briefcase or pair of glasses, turn them in to the Lost and Found, or make an effort to find the owner.

*W*hen the elevator is crowded and you're at the front, step off and give the person in a rush your space. Use the time while you wait for the next elevator to take a deep breath and count your blessings.

BE AN ANGEL TO PASSERSBY

●●●

*B*e attentive to the needs of others. Lend a helping hand whenever possible. Remember the times when an anonymous soul assisted you.

●●●

*W*hen your grocery cart is full and the person behind you with only a few purchases looks tired and hurried, let him go ahead of you. A thoughtful act like this, at just the right moment, can transform a passerby's mood from grouchy to grateful.

●●●

*S*ometimes we move through the day in a fog and forget the power of a smile. Smile at those you come in contact with throughout the day; it's something that is usually returned.

●●●

LOVING-KINDNESS WILL HEAL OUR PLANET AND SPREAD PEACE.

BE AN ANGEL TO PASSERSBY

IT HAS BEEN SAID THAT TO LOOK INTO A PERSON'S LEFT EYE IS TO SEE THEIR SOUL. TRY LOOKING INTO THE LEFT EYES OF PEOPLE WHO CROSS YOUR PATH. TRY CONNECTING WITH THE UNIVERSAL ENERGY WE ALL SHARE.

● ● ●

*R*escue the dropped pacifier, billfold, car keys— anything that can be immediately returned to the passerby.

● ● ●

*P*lease, thank you, excuse me, are simple phrases that say "I respect you." Use them generously.

● ● ●

DO ALL THE GOOD YOU CAN,
BY ALL THE MEANS YOU CAN,
IN ALL THE WAYS YOU CAN,
IN ALL THE PLACES YOU CAN,
AT ALL THE TIMES YOU CAN.
TO ALL THE PEOPLE YOU CAN,
AS LONG AS YOU CAN.
—JOHN WESLEY'S RULE

RECIOUS

THE
ANGEL
OF
FRIENDS

Friendships are a specialty for Precious. Her mission is to foster relationships between kindred spirits. A cape of many colors, to represent the myriad of individuals in the world, is her garment. She is a weaver of like souls. She carries a pouch of silver and gold thread for binding together interconnections between mortals.

Precious is found on planes and trains. She encourages introductions between travelers. The friendship angel visits schools and offices and will often cause two people literally to bump into each other, a precious way to begin a friendship. Our angel of friends is found wherever there is potential for linking like souls together.

Once the friendship has begun, Precious starts to weave her tapestry of shared experiences that bind the friends to one another. Each relationship is unique in design and purpose. There are friends who become companions, confidants, playmates, and supporters. Precious receives divine guidance for selecting the appropriate person to fulfill a specific need. Her sense of timing plays a very important role when creating new comraderies. When she hears a mortal say, "I need a friend," Precious moves quickly, with deliberation.

The angel of friends is truly a matchmaker. You will recognize her the next time you are somewhere and you hear an inner voice say, "Go ahead, introduce yourself. You just might meet a Precious friend."

BE AN ANGEL TO YOUR FRIENDS

"THERE IS A
MAGNET IN YOUR
HEART THAT WILL
ATTRACT TRUE
FRIENDS. THAT
MAGNET IS
UNSELFISHNESS,
THINKING OF
OTHERS
FIRST . . . WHEN
YOU LEARN TO LIVE
FOR OTHERS, THEY
WILL LIVE FOR YOU."
—PARAMAHANSA
YOGANANDA

*C*arve out time to truly "be" with your friend. A long chat over coffee in the afternoon. A walk in the park. An evening at your house catching up over supper.

*C*reate a handmade card and decorate the envelope with glitter. Sign it, "From someone who thinks you're great!"

*F*or a friend's birthday create a basket filled with little things she loves: candies, flower seeds, a special tape of show tunes, a photo of the two of you in a tiny frame, and an invitation to lunch.

*M*editate on what it means to be a friend.

BE AN ANGEL TO YOUR FRIENDS

Keep a list of important anniversaries in your friend's life. For instance, the day when you became friends, the day she got her new cat, the day she started her new job, etc. Send little notes to celebrate these special times.

Be a good listener. Listen with an open mind and heart and a closed mouth.

Cherish your friends. Nurture your friendships with honesty and devotion.

Call a friend whose soul needs soothing. Pack some oranges and cookies and go walking together. Share the sights, the sounds, the smells of a sunny afternoon.

CREATE A "BLESSINGS BOX" FOR A FRIEND. PAINT OR COLLAGE A SMALL BOX. FILL IT WITH TREASURES—A GOOD LUCK CHARM, INCENSE, A POEM, ETC. BE CREATIVE! ENCLOSE A CARD EXPLAINING THE MEANING OF EACH TOKEN.

IV
THE ANGELS OF SPECIAL NEEDS AND OCCASIONS

WE ARE SURROUNDED BY OUR ANGELIC COMPANIONS
TWENTY-FOUR HOURS A DAY. HOWEVER, THERE ARE TIMES
IN OUR LIVES WHEN WE ARE MOST AWARE OF THE ANGELS'
PRESENCE. THESE ARE THE GUARDIANS WHO EMBRACE US DURING
TIMES OF CRISIS, TRANSITION, AND JOY.

HOPE
THE ANGEL OF THE HOMELESS

COMFORT
THE ANGEL OF THE SICK

WANDER
THE ANGEL OF THE TRAVELER

FAITH
THE ANGEL OF THE DYING

FESTIVITY
THE ANGEL OF CELEBRATIONS

HOPE

THE
ANGEL
OF
THE HOMELESS

Hope, the nomad angel, moves from place to place. She is plain and simple in appearance; her aura is golden and warm; her beauty lies within her. Hope's presence nurtures the human spirit. The angel of the homeless moves throughout our cities, tending the wanderers, the misplaced, the young and old who for a myriad of reasons find themselves living on the streets.

Hope watches over her charges with loving attention. Lovingly, she directs them to food and shelter. When the weather is frigid, she ignites dreams of warmer places for relief. She whispers in the ears of passersby to open their hearts and to share their talents and treasures with their fellow human beings.

Hope is the angel of encouragement.
Gently she nudges and guides these
searching souls. She encourages them not to
give up or give in to despair. Sometimes she is the link
between the homeless person and one who is more
fortunate. When this wondrous miracle occurs, lives
are changed, both lives, and the world becomes a little
brighter . . . there's Hope.

BE AN ANGEL TO THE HOMELESS

> "A DECENT PROVISION FOR THE POOR IS THE TRUE TEST OF CIVILIZATION."
> —SAMUEL JOHNSON

> "ALL THE LONELY PEOPLE, WHERE DO THEY ALL BELONG?"
> —PAUL McCARTNEY AND JOHN LENNON
> "ELEANOR RIGBY"

*D*onate usable items you no longer need to your local shelter. All of us have things in cupboards and closets that we never touch but that could be very important to someone less fortunate.

*M*ake up little angel packages to distribute on the streets when approached by the homeless. These tiny bundles might include one or more of the following: sample-size tubes of toothpaste, soap, a toothbrush, a comb, small packages of tissues, lotion, apples, oranges, socks, gloves, etc.

BE AN ANGEL TO THE HOMELESS

*R*emember the homeless child. Make small giveaway packages of picture books, crayons and paper, small toys, socks, underwear, disposable diapers, baby lotion, baby food.

*V*olunteer at your local shelter. Reach out to others, serve a meal, share your love and energy.

*U*se your talents and skills, open your heart, discover your own special way of sharing with your fellow human beings. Discover your angel within.

"FREELY WE SERVE,
BECAUSE WE FREELY
LOVE, AS IN OUR
WILL
TO LOVE OR NOT;
IN THIS WE STAND
OR FALL."
—JOHN MILTON

HOPE GIVES HOPE.

BE AN ANGEL TO THE HOMELESS

THE ANGEL OF
THE HOMELESS GETS
INVOLVED.

"THERE ARE SO
MANY HUNGRY
PEOPLE THAT GOD
CANNOT APPEAR TO
THEM EXCEPT IN
THE FORM OF
BREAD."
—CORITA KENT

*G*ather several friends together and adopt a family in need. Share the responsibility of providing food, clothing, finding appropriate shelter, schools for the children, job search, etc. Help turn someone's life around.

*R*emember the homeless during the holidays. In the true spirit of giving, invite your family, your children, your friends to go gift shopping for a local shelter. Purchase blankets, toys, or clothes and then deliver them where they will be properly distributed.

COMFORT

Comfort is the angel of compassion and healing. She is
infused with pink light, and her wings are swift and
silent. Her deep blue eyes reflect the benevolence of
heaven, and her angel voice manifests tones that reach
the deepest levels of mortal understanding.

Comfort is found wherever there is human suffering.
She is attuned to the diseases that attack the body,
mind, and spirit. Physical illness finds Comfort at the
bedsides of those undergoing treatment, receiving
transplants, and recovering from surgery and all other
ailments.

The healing angel attends the weary in need of renewal
for the psyche and soul. She offers hope and

consolation to mortals desperate from the traumas of a difficult life. Comfort brings peace to the ravaged heart and confused mind.

She embraces the starving, soothes the battered, and sustains those who suffer with AIDS. Comfort is an angel of mercy, always uplifting and offering restoration of the spirit even when a cure may not be possible.

She knows that the healing of our planet must begin with our willingness to acknowledge and confront the suffering of the world. We must also become angels of mercy.

Comfort supports the caregivers of the earth's sick. They are likely to feel her presence, her sustenance, her grace, as they go about their blessed work.

BE AN ANGEL TO THE SICK

A GENTLE VOICE
CAN HEAL.

"ILLNESS IS THE
NIGHT-SIDE OF LIFE,
A MORE ONEROUS
CITIZENSHIP.
EVERYONE WHO IS
BORN HOLDS DUAL
CITIZENSHIP, IN THE
KINGDOM OF THE
WELL AND IN THE
KINGDOM OF THE
SICK."
—SUSAN SONTAG

*V*olunteer to visit the sick at your local hospital. Your duties might include reading to children in the pediatric ward, or delivering flowers and mail to patients in their rooms. A smiling face and the touch of a hand are powerful medicine that you can provide.

*W*hen someone you know is going to have surgery, prepare a basket of reading material and fruit, snacks, etc., to support the family members while they wait for news from the doctor on the day of the surgery.

*O*ffer to relieve someone who is caring for a sick relative. An hour or two away from responsibilities can offer a new lease on life to a caregiver.

BE AN ANGEL TO THE SICK

*B*ecome educated about AIDS. Volunteer to answer phones for your local AIDS hotline. Awareness and education are vital to stopping the spread of AIDS. You can make a difference.

*T*he Red Cross offers courses in first aid, CPR, and disaster training. Knowing these skills might enable you to save a life.

*I*f a friend is ill and unable to attend her child's school program, dance recital, soccer game, etc., offer to attend and photograph or videotape it for her.

COMFORT BRINGS COMFORT WHEREVER SHE GOES.

BE AWARE OF THE SUFFERING IN OUR WORLD. REACH OUT!

BE AN ANGEL TO THE SICK

> "THE QUALITY OF
> MERCY IS NOT
> STRAIN'D,
> IT DROPPETH AS THE
> GENTLE RAIN FROM
> HEAVEN
> UPON THE PLACE
> BENEATH: IT IS
> TWICE BLESS'D;
> IT BLESSETH HIM
> THAT GIVES AND
> HIM THAT
> TAKES. . . ."
> —WILLIAM SHAKESPEAR

*F*or someone down with the flu or the sniffles, offer to pick up prescriptions and extra tissues.

*W*hen you're sure there's nothing you can do to help someone, do the greatest thing you can do . . . pray for them.

*C*reate a box of cheer for someone going into the hospital. Individually wrap a small bottle of lotion, a little book of poems, a handmade good luck charm, etc., one for each day in the hospital. Attach little notes of encouragement. Present these charming gifts in a decorative container.

WANDER

THE

ANGEL

OF

THE TRAVELER

Wander accompanies the traveler on his journeys. His garment is wrinkle resistant. He travels light. Wings with great strength carry him long distances. His halo is bright, to provide a beacon to those who need help finding their way. Protection and assistance are the chief responsibilities of this angel.

Wander gives the traveler a sudden boost of energy to catch nearly missed planes and trains. He whispers a reminder to collect all belongings when checking out of hotel rooms. This tireless angel arranges chance meetings that become love affairs and lifelong friendships.

Safekeeping is foremost in Wander's mind. He snatches the traveler from curbs to save him from the oncoming traffic. Wander whispers gently to the sleeping vacationing sunbather to awake before the sunlight can do its damage. And he rides next to the white-knuckled flyer and provides reassurance during takeoff.

Wander, the angel of the traveler, wanders the world with purpose and resourcefulness. You'll recognize him in human form the next time you're traveling and looking for directions and someone says, "You look lost, may I help you find your way?"

BE AN ANGEL TO THE TRAVELER

SPREAD SMILES
WHEREVER YOU
TRAVEL!

"FOLLOWING THE
SUN WE LEFT THE
OLD WORLD."
—INSCRIPTION ON ONE OF
COLUMBUS'S CARAVELS

*I*n airports and train stations be aware of luggage and belongings left behind. Deliver them to the Lost and Found or call them to the attention of the forgetful traveler.

*W*hen a guest comes to stay in your home, provide some special touches in their room: stationery, fresh flowers, music, a tiny "welcome" gift. Create a home away from home.

*W*hen traveling, assist the elderly with their luggage.

BE AN ANGEL TO THE TRAVELER

*P*ack a goody bag for a friend's small child to carry on a travel day. Include a coloring book, crayons, stickers, a small puzzle, and healthy treats. These simple items can provide hours of entertainment for a restless little traveler.

*G*ive a tissue and a smile to the teary-eyed person next to you on the plane who has just said good-bye to their sweetheart.

*C*reate a map library of places you've been to share with traveling friends.

CALL ON WANDER WHEN YOU'VE LOST YOUR WAY.

"THERE IS NO UNHAPPINESS LIKE THE MISERY OF SIGHTING LAND AGAIN AFTER A CHEERFUL, CARELESS VOYAGE."
—MARK TWAIN

BE AN ANGEL TO THE TRAVELER

MAKE NEW FRIENDS
THE WORLD OVER.

SPREAD PEACE AND
GOODWILL.

CREATE A TRAVEL JOURNAL.

SELECT A SMALL BLANK BOOK TO USE AS A PLACE TO
RECORD YOUR THOUGHTS, FEELINGS, EXPERIENCES AS
YOU JOURNEY. THE BOOK SHOULD BE SMALL
ENOUGH TO CARRY WITH YOU AT ALL TIMES.
SIDEWALK CAFÉS, MUSEUM BENCHES, AND CITY
PARKS ARE INSPIRATIONAL PLACES FOR JOURNALING.
YOU MIGHT LIKE TO TAKE A SMALL SET OF
WATERCOLORS OR COLORED PENCILS FOR CREATING
TINY SKETCHES OF THE SIGHTS. USE ADJECTIVES
FREELY WHEN RECORDING YOUR IMPRESSIONS. BE
DESCRIPTIVE AS YOU WRITE ABOUT YOUR
MEANDERINGS. COLLECT POSTCARDS, NAPKINS,
TICKET STUBS, AND OTHER SOUVENIRS TO ADD TO
YOUR BOOK OF MEMORIES. WHEN YOU RETURN
HOME YOU MIGHT WISH TO INCLUDE A PHOTO OR
TWO TO HELP YOU RECALL YOUR JOURNEY.

FAITH

THE ANGEL OF THE DYING

Acceptance and peace arrive on wings of Faith. She is the angel of pure white light. Her brilliance floods the hearts, minds, and souls of those who witness her presence. Her wings are white with dove feathers, and her halo is golden like the sun. Faith's eyes reflect the tranquillity of heaven, and her touch provides release from the physical world.

The angel of the dying appears to those souls returning to the spirit world from this mortal experience. It is a time of remembering the home from which one came. It is a time of reconnecting with the light body, the form of formlessness. Faith is the facilitator for this miraculous process. She assists God as a messenger of the beauty and joy that awaits.

The angel of eternal peace acts as a midwife. She is present to attend the birth into light and renewal. It is Faith who gathers family and friends on the other side to call to the one between two worlds. They are beckoned by Faith to reassure and welcome the departing soul.

Fear cannot stand in the presence of Faith. Her light overpowers the darkness. She is a welcome sight to those who have suffered and fought the good fight. Faith is a merciful presence to the soul who departs this world suddenly, without warning.

The angel of light holds out her hand reassuringly. Her compassion and gentleness speak without words. She waits for the sign from the divine and at that moment, in a heartbeat, she carries the soul home with Faith.

BE AN ANGEL TO THE DYING

*B*ecome a hospice volunteer. Hospice programs provide a variety of services and opportunities for outreach to the dying and their caregivers.

*W*hen death is imminent for a loved one, provide reassurance that it is all right to move on. Mention the names of family and friends who have gone before. These things may be said even when the person is unconscious. Love and peace are received beyond the physical body.

"LIFE IS A GREAT SURPRISE. I DO NOT SEE WHY DEATH SHOULD NOT BE AN EVEN GREATER ONE."
—VLADIMIR NABOKOV

*P*rovide support to the caregiver of someone who is dying. Don't be concerned about what to say. A loving presence and outstretched hand speak beyond words.

BE AN ANGEL TO THE DYING

*V*olunteer at your local nursing home. Often an elderly person has no family nearby at the time of dying. We don't have to know someone to hold their hand or offer prayers for a peaceful transition.

*H*elp a dying person put their final affairs in order. Offer to write letters, arrange a will, or take care of anything that might cause the person anguish or worry.

*T*ell family and friends, "I love you." Express your feelings today. Cherish life.

"I LOOKED OVER JORDAN, AND WHAT DID I SEE? . . . A BAND OF ANGELS COMING AFTER ME, COMING FOR TO CARRY ME HOME."
—"SWING LOW, SWEET CHARIOT"

BE AN ANGEL TO THE DYING

"DEATH IS SIMPLY A SHEDDING OF THE PHYSICAL BODY, LIKE THE BUTTERFLY COMING OUT OF A COCOON. . . . IT'S LIKE PUTTING AWAY YOUR WINTER COAT WHEN SPRING COMES."
—ELISABETH KÜBLER-ROSS

IF YOU HAVE LOST A LOVED ONE, CREATE A SPECIAL SHRINE ON A TABLE IN YOUR HOME. PLACE ON IT A PICTURE OF THE PERSON WHO HAS DIED; ADD FLOWERS AND A CANDLE. WRITE A LETTER TO YOUR LOVED ONE EXPRESSING YOUR GRIEF AND PLACE IT ON THE TABLE. LET THIS SHRINE BE A FOCAL POINT FOR YOUR GRIEVING, A PLACE TO CRY, TO PRAY, TO REFLECT AND PROCESS YOUR FEELINGS. AS TIME HEALS THE INITIAL PAIN, YOU MAY WISH TO BURN YOUR GRIEF LETTER AS A SYMBOL THAT YOUR PERIOD OF MOURNING HAS ENDED. YOU MIGHT TAKE THE ASHES FROM YOUR LETTER AND ADD THEM TO THE EARTH OUTSIDE IN YOUR GARDEN WHERE YOU PLANT A SMALL TREE IN MEMORY OF THE ONE WHO HAS DIED. THIS SYMBOLIZES THAT EVERYTHING CHANGES AND LIFE CONTINUES.

FESTIVITY

THE
ANGEL
OF
CELEBRATIONS

Dazzling colored ribbons flow from Festivity's robes. Fuchsia, turquoise, and amber bands of light frame his aura. Merriment and whimsy are his calling cards, and he wears a wreath of stars in his curly white hair. Wings of gold and silver illuminate his shoulders.

His joyful appearance reveals his ability to spread delight wherever he goes. Festivity helps blow out candles on birthday cakes. He joins Tender, the angel of the beloved, on anniversaries and at weddings to spread romance and the smell of roses.

There are special celebrations that call for Festivity's presence. The promotion at the office, the arrival of a new baby, the first flowers of spring, a good report

card—these occasions call for
the angel of celebrations.
Whenever mortals gather to
share good news, Festivity is there.

The festive angel also adds a celebratory feeling to the
tiny moments of the day that are rich with cause for
merrymaking. A child tying her shoe for the first time,
the sight of a beautiful sunset, or a chance reunion
with an old friend—these are special happenings that
invoke a pause to enjoy the preciousness of life.
Festivity is there at lightning speed to deliver
a feeling of joy and excitement.

Holidays, birthdays, anniversaries, and
all the blithesome instances in between
create the connecting fiber of our lives. These are
causes for celebration and opportunities for Festivity.

BE AN ANGEL AT CELEBRATIONS

> "LET US EAT AND
> DRINK; FOR
> TOMORROW WE
> SHALL DIE."
> —ISAIAH 22:13

*L*ook for any cause for celebration. The changing seasons, a move to a new apartment, the recovery from an illness, an unexpected visitor—these moments create potential for a special meal, a distinctive gift, or picture taking.

*S*tart a celebration scrapbook for your family. Collect invitations, photos, and memorabilia from holidays, birthdays, etc. Write about your feelings and memories of the special occasions.

*F*estivity arrives in a burst of color!

BE AN ANGEL AT CELEBRATIONS

*C*elebrate the wonders of nature: a new litter of kittens, the blooming crocus in spring, the autumn sunset.

*W*hen sending a greeting card to a friend, add confetti or glitter, decorate the envelope with rubber stamps or markers. Add a festive touch to herald the joyful message inside.

*L*eave an anonymous remembrance on a co-worker's desk, a friend's front porch, a child's schoolbag. Attach a note that simply says: "I celebrate YOU."

"COOKING IS LIKE LOVE. IT SHOULD BE ENTERED INTO WITH ABANDON OR NOT AT ALL."
—COLETTE

TREAT EACH MEAL AS CAUSE FOR CELEBRATION. GIVE THANKS FOR THE BOUNTY.

BE AN ANGEL AT CELEBRATIONS

> "THE HOLIEST OF
> ALL HOLIDAYS ARE
> THOSE
> KEPT BY OURSELVES
> IN SILENCE AND
> APART;
> THE SECRET
> ANNIVERSARIES OF
> THE HEART."
> —HENRY WADSWORTH
> LONGFELLOW

CELEBRATE LIFE'S TRANSITIONS

TO COMMEMORATE A BIRTH, PRESENT THE NEW PARENTS WITH A TREE FOR PLANTING. THIS SYMBOLIZES THE BEGINNING OF LIFE AND A WAY TO MARK THE YEARS AS THEIR CHILD GROWS.

CELEBRATE A YOUNG PERSON'S THIRTEENTH BIRTHDAY WITH THE PRESENTATION OF A "THINGS I WANT YOU TO KNOW" BOOK. ASK FAMILY AND FRIENDS TO CONTRIBUTE PERSONAL STORIES, REFLECTIONS, AND WORDS OF WISDOM. ASK THE ELDERS IN THE FAMILY TO TELL THEIR STORIES ON AUDIO OR VIDEO TAPE. PRESENT THE BRIDE AND GROOM WITH PHOTO ALBUMS FROM EACH FAMILY. INCLUDE NAMES, BIRTHDAYS, FAMOUS FAMILY QUOTES, RECIPES, AND TRADITIONS AS A WELCOMING INTRODUCTION TO THEIR NEW LIFE TOGETHER.

A FEW CLOSING THOUGHTS

*N*ow that you have become acquainted with the angels all around you, be aware of how they move throughout your life. Notice the blessings you receive during the day. Invite the angels to speak with you by allowing quiet time for prayer and meditation. Listen for their guidance wherever you may be.

*R*emember that through caring, sharing, and reaching out to others you are making a difference in our world. You are helping our heavenly friends to heal our planet. Open your eyes, your ears, your heart, and be aware of ways that you too may *Be an Angel!*